AIR FRYER FOR ONE

COOKBOOK

Healthy, Quick and Easy Recipes for Cooking for One Person in Your Air Fryer

CHRISTOPHER LESTER

CONTENTS

Poultry & Meat

Sides & Vegetables

Desserts

4

WELCOME

Welcome to the world of air frying, one delicious dish after another. Cooking for yourself has never been so easy, efficient, and enjoyable. Suppose you are a lone cook who wants to prepare mouthwatering meals without the hassle. In that case, this cookbook will be your key to unlocking a world of flavor while keeping portion sizes in mind.

The Air Fryer is your trusty kitchen helper, and we're here to help you make the most of it. In these pages, you'll find a treasure trove of recipes for the air fryer, carefully designed for one person. No more worrying about leftovers or reducing recipes - every dish you'll find here is a masterpiece with perfect portions.

Cooking for one person with an air fryer is the perfect combination of convenience, speed, and utility. With virtually no oil required, you'll achieve the coveted crispy crust. An air fryer can make everything from a quick weeknight meal to a gourmet treat for two, and you'll soon become a pro at preparing these delicious dishes.

This cookbook provides step-by-step instructions, pro tips, and advice on preparing dishes according to your taste preferences. We aim to make your self-cooking experience easy, enjoyable, and rewarding.

WHAT EXACTLY IS AN AIR FRYER?

An air fryer is essentially an enhanced, compact convection oven that finds its place on your kitchen countertop. This ingenious kitchen appliance is designed to fry various foods, such as meats, potato chips, and even healthier pastries, without excessive oil. Think of it as a mini-convection oven dedicated to frying, capable of delivering the same delightful taste and texture you'd expect from deep-fried dishes but with a significant reduction in fat content and calorie count.

HOW DOES IT WORK?

An air fryer operates by circulating heated air at a specific temperature, directing it around the food while transforming any moisture into a fine mist. In the heated chamber, dry heat penetrates the food, ensuring it attains the same crispy texture associated with deep-fried cuisine. This process triggers a chemical reaction known as the Maillard effect, where sugars and amino acids interact when subjected to heat. Consequently, this reaction not only imparts a color change but also enhances the flavor profile of the food.

The air fryer's cooking zone is designed to disperse hot air in all directions, ensuring even cooking on all sides. What sets an air fryer apart from a conventional oven is the rapid airflow inside, which exceeds that of a standard oven. The compact cooking chamber of an air fryer accelerates the cooking process, delivering efficiently prepared meals.

Air-fried cuisine is a healthier alternative to deep-fried foods due to its reduced fat and calorie content. Unlike deep frying, which submerges food in copious amounts of oil, air frying requires only a minimal drizzle of oil to achieve a comparable texture and flavor. In fact, some air fryer manufacturers claim that this method can cut the fat content of fried food by as much as 75%.

The beauty of an air fryer lies in its versatility. You can recreate the taste of deep-fried dishes with an air fryer, and it effortlessly takes on tasks typically reserved for a conventional oven, offering an enhanced cooking experience.

THE ADVANTAGES OF USING AN AIR FRYER

- **Quick Meal Preparation**: Air fryers excel at preparing meals swiftly thanks to their compact cooking chamber and efficient fan-driven air circulation. While traditional ovens may take 20-30 minutes to preheat, air fryers reach desired high temperatures within minutes of being switched on.

- **Healthier Cooking:** Traditional deep-frying often requires copious amounts of cooking oil, which can introduce harmful elements to your food. In contrast, air fryers allow for cooking with minimal or no oil, delivering the same crispy texture as traditionally fried dishes. Whether onion rings, frozen fries, or wings, you can savor the crunch without the extra calories and fat.

- **Versatility:** The culinary possibilities with an air fryer are nearly endless. It outperforms ovens in frying and healthy cooking and can also roast, bake, broil, and grill. From frozen to fresh ingredients, an air fryer handles them easily, making it a convenient appliance for reheating leftovers.

- **Space Efficiency:** Air fryers are space-savers in the kitchen. They are compact and take up minimal counter space, making them a suitable addition to any kitchen.

- **Ease of Use:** Operating an air fryer is a breeze. Simply plug it in, add ingredients, choose your desired cooking temperature and time, and press start. There's no need for constant stirring, as you might with stovetop cooking.

- **Effortless Cleanup:** Cleaning an air fryer is a cinch. With removable, non-stick-coated baskets and pans, food residue doesn't stick, and cleanup takes minutes.

- **Energy Efficiency:** Air fryers are more energy-efficient than traditional ovens and won't heat up your kitchen as ovens often do. An air fryer is a smart idea if you want to save on your electric bill or maintain a cooler cooking environment.

MAINTAINING YOUR AIR FRYER FOR LONG-LASTING PERFORMANCE

The air fryer is a valuable assistant in your kitchen, simplifying the cooking process and increasing convenience. However, regular maintenance is essential to guarantee its durability and optimal performance to prevent malfunctions and damage. Here's what's involved:

- **Allow Adequate Space:** Position your air fryer with at least four inches of clearance on all sides and above it. This space is crucial for safety and optimal performance as it allows the release of vapor during cooking. Placing the air fryer in a confined space may lead to overheating.

- **Inspect the Power Cord:** Always ensure the power cord is in good condition before plugging it in. Connecting a damaged cord to an outlet can potentially cause sparks, posing risks of a kitchen fire, injuries, or worse. Check for any signs of damage, including exposed wires, before using your air fryer.

- **Regularly Examine Components**: Before each use, conduct a thorough inspection of all air fryer components, including the frying pan, basket, and handle. If you discover any broken or damaged parts, promptly contact the store where you made the purchase or reach out to the manufacturer to arrange for replacements.

- **Steady Placement:** Place your air fryer on a flat, stable surface, ensuring it stands upright before you start preparing your food.

- **Clean and Maintain:** Ensure the air fryer is in good condition and free of debris before use, especially if unused for a while. Over time, it may accumulate dust or dirt. In the event of food residue or other contaminants on the pan or basket, cleaning them thoroughly before commencing your cooking session is advisable.

HELPFUL TIPS FOR MASTERING AIR FRYING

- **Avoid Overcrowding:** Resist the urge to overpack the cooking basket. While it may seem like a time-saver, overcrowding leads to uneven cooking and insufficient crispiness. Give your ingredients the space they need for perfect results.

- **Add Water for Fatty Foods:** When preparing fatty foods like sausages, bacon, or burgers, consider adding a small amount of water to the air fryer drawer just beneath the cooking basket. This prevents the oil from overheating and smoking, ensuring a more pleasant cooking experience.

- **Secure Light Foods:** Air fryer fans can sometimes blow around lightweight ingredients. To prevent this, use toothpicks to secure items like smaller vegetables or delicate items.

- **Check Doneness as Needed:** One of the perks of air frying is the ability to check on your food without disrupting the cooking process. Feel free to open the air fryer drawer as often as required to assess your meal's progress. Most air fryers will either pause heating while the drawer is open, then resume when closed, or continue cooking while keeping track of the cooking time.

- **Spritz with Oil:** For a beautifully browned and crispy finish, consider spritzing your food with oil during cooking. This not only enhances browning but also promotes even crisping.

- **Flip Foods Halfway:** Just as you would on a grill or deep-frying, remember to flip your food over halfway through the cooking time. This ensures that both sides brown evenly, resulting in a delightful texture.

- **Shake the Basket**: To distribute the ingredients evenly and encourage more uniform browning and crisping, give the cooking basket a gentle shake several times during the cooking process. This simple step can significantly affect the outcome of your air-fried dishes.

Appetizers & Snacks

Potato Wedges

Servings: 1 • **Prep time:** 5 minutes (plus 20 minutes for soaking) • **Cook Time:** 15 minutes

I use this dish as both a snack and a garnish. It all depends on the frying time and the frequency of shaking. You can also add potato wedges as an ingredient for a cheese and cream casserole.

The potatoes can be peeled, but if you leave a little peel on, the dish looks like a comfort food. Try replacing the spices with a handful of fresh sage and thyme, which give the dish a French charm.

Sauce options: classic ketchup, garlic or truffle aioli, chipotle mayo, ranch dressing, cheese sauce, honey mustard sauce.

INGREDIENTS

1-2 medium-sized waxy potatoes
1 tsp. olive oil
¼ tsp. smoked paprika/cayenne pepper

¼ tsp. garlic powder
Salt (optional)
2 Tbsp. Sriracha hot chili sauce

HOW TO COOK

1. Wash and scrub the potatoes thoroughly. There's no need to peel them. Cut the potatoes into even slices using a mandoline slicer or a sharp knife. The thinner you can slice them, the crispier your wedges will be.
2. Place the potato slices in a bowl of cold water for about 20 minutes. This removes excess starch from the potato and results in crispier wedges.
3. Drain the potato wedges and pat them dry.
4. Toss the prepared potato wedges with olive oil, seasonings of your choice, and salt, if desired.
5. Meanwhile, preheat your air fryer to 360 - 375°F (180 - 190°C).
6. Place the potato slices in a single layer in the air fryer basket. Cook for 10-15 minutes, flipping them or shaking the basket every 5 minutes. Keep a close eye on them to prevent overcooking.
7. They are done when they reach your desired level of crispiness. Some slices may cook faster than others, so remove them as they become ready.
8. Transfer the wedges to a cooling rack or a paper towel to cool and become crispier. Season with additional salt or seasonings if needed.
9. Serve with Sriracha hot sauce or sauce of your choice.

NUTRITION INFO (Per Serving)

Calories: 481, Total Fat: 25 g, Saturated Fat: 8 g, Cholesterol: 469 mg, Sodium: 297 mg, Total Carbs: 40 g, Fiber: 6 g, Sugar: 6 g, Protein: 25 g, Potassium: 1143 mg

Mozzarella Sticks

Servings: 1 • **Prep time:** 7 minutes (plus 30 minutes for freezing) • **Cook Time:** 7 minutes

Want something cheesy, gooey, and yummy?! This recipe is easy to put into action even on busy afternoons. For a gluten-free or low-carb option, use almond flour. It gives a nutty flavor that pairs perfectly with the mozzarella.

If you freeze the mozzarella sticks before coating and frying they will not melt in the hot air.

Sauce options: buffalo sauce, sriracha mayo, garlic aioli.

INGREDIENTS

3 mozzarella string cheese sticks, cut in half
3 Tbsp. all-purpose flour
1 small egg, whisked
½ cup breadcrumbs
1 Tbsp. Parmesan, grated

¼ tsp. dried thyme
¼ tsp. dried rosemary
¼ tsp. garlic powder
Olive oil spray
Marinara sauce, for serving

HOW TO COOK

1. Place the all-purpose flour in one bowl. Pour the whisked egg into another bowl. Mix the breadcrumbs, Parmesan cheese, dried herbs, and garlic powder in the third bowl.
2. Cover each mozzarella stick with flour. Then, dip it into the whisked egg, allowing any excess to drip off. Finally, coat the stick in the breadcrumb mixture. Double-coat the mozzarella sticks by dipping them back into the egg and breadcrumb mixture.
3. Place the sticks on a sheet lined with parchment paper and freeze them for 30 - 35 minutes. Freezing helps the cheese hold its shape while air frying.
4. Meanwhile, preheat your air fryer to 390°F (200°C).
5. Lightly grease the air fryer basket and the frozen mozzarella sticks with cooking spray. Arrange them in a single layer in the basket, ensuring they don't touch.
6. Cook the mozzarella sticks for 5-7 minutes until golden brown and crispy. Be cautious not to overcook them, as the cheese may start to ooze out.
7. Let them stand for 1-2 minutes before serving with marinara sauce or dipping sauce of your choice.

NUTRITION INFO (Per Serving)

Calories: 608, Total Fat: 22.9 g, Saturated Fat: 13 g, Cholesterol: 230 mg, Sodium: 1197 mg, Total Carbs: 62 g, Fiber: 4 g, Sugar: 4 g, Protein: 32 g

Nut Cocktail

Servings: 1 cup • **Prep time:** 5 minutes • **Cook Time:** 6 minutes

Even if you prepare nuts without any additives, the dish will still turn out infinitely delicious. Frying nuts caramelize their own sugars. You can use whatever nuts you have on hand and finish the dish off. A crunchy sugar coating and a little spice make them not too sweet and not too spicy.

Serve them with smoothies or other appetizers - they go fast, so make a spare. Add seeds to the mix: sunflower seeds, pumpkin seeds, and sesame seeds all add flavor and texture.

INGREDIENTS

1 cup (130 g) raw almonds/pecans/walnuts/cashew

For sweet nuts (optional):
white/brown sugar
ground cinnamon
pumpkin pie spices

For savory nuts (optional):
herbs
ground nutmeg
oriental spices/curry
onion/garlic powder
chili powder
olive oil/melted salted butter/coconut oil

HOW TO COOK

1. Combine nuts with your favorite sweet or savory seasoning.
2. Preheat your air fryer to 350°F (180°C).
3. Arrange nuts in a single layer in the air fryer basket and fry for 5 - 6 minutes, shaking the basket every 2 minutes.
4. Cool completely before serving.
5. Serve with soups, salads, breakfast porridge, or as a snack.

NUTRITION INFO (Per Serving)

Calories: 789, Total Carbohydrates: 28.1 g, Total Fat: 70 g, Cholesterol 0 mg, Sodium 2 mg, Protein: 28.1 g, Fiber: 17 g, Sugar: 6 g

Onion Rings

Servings: 1 • **Prep time:** 10 minutes • **Cook Time:** 10 minutes

It is important to get the right consistency of batter in this recipe. Add 1-2 tablespoons of flour if the batter is too runny or sour cream if the batter is too thick. The onion rings should hold their shape and not spread out.

There is a classic recipe of batter for onion rings made of milk, egg, breadcrumbs, and flour. But I suggest you try a more savory recipe. It is absolutely just as simple and easy to make after a busy day.

Sauce options: sweet chili sauce, ranch dressing, cheese sauce, honey mustard sauce.

INGREDIENTS

1 sweet onion (Vidalia/Walla Walla), peeled
Olive oil as needed
1 whole egg, whisked
1/8 tsp. cayenne pepper
¼ tsp. garlic powder
½ cup (60 g) all-purpose flour

1/8 tsp. black pepper
1/8 tsp. smoked paprika
1/8 tsp. salt
2 Tbsp. mayonnaise
1 Tbsp. ketchup
1 Tbsp. sour cream

HOW TO COOK

1. Slice the onions into ½-inch-diameter rings, then separate the rings. The small inner rings can be used for other recipes.
2. In one bowl, mix all the ingredients for the sauce. In another bowl, place the beaten egg.
3. Dip each onion ring into the beaten egg. Then, dip the ring thoroughly into the sauce mixture. Repeat this process for all the onion rings.
4. Meanwhile, preheat the air fryer to 375°F (190°C).
5. Lightly spray the air fryer basket and onion rings with cooking spray. Arrange the rings in the basket in a single layer.
6. Cook the onion rings for 8-10 minutes, turning them over halfway through. They should be golden brown and crispy.
7. Serve hot with your favorite sauce, ranch dressing, or spicy mayonnaise.

NUTRITION INFO (Per Serving)

Calories: 191, Total Fat: 0.9 g, Saturated Fat: 0 g, Cholesterol: 0 mg, Sodium: 288.9 mg, Total Carbs: 23 g, Fiber: 2 g, Sugar: 4 g, Protein: 6 g, Potassium: 181 mg

Jalapeño Poppers

Servings: 1 • **Prep time:** 10 minutes • **Cook Time:** 12 minutes

These bacon-wrapped jalapeño peppers are a fantastic appetizer to make ahead of time. Just follow the recipe instructions to stuff and wrap the peppers. Instead of cooking them right away, place them in the refrigerator. When you're ready to serve, simply air fry them and enjoy! They will be a bit softer after baking if that works for you.

You can customize the filling by adding garlic/onion powder, bacon bits, or finely chopped onions. Use gloves when removing seeds from peppers to avoid irritation.

INGREDIENTS

2-3 fresh jalapeno peppers
2 Tbsp. cream cheese, softened
2 Tbsp. Cheddar cheese, grated
¼ tsp. garlic powder
¼ tsp. onion powder

1/8 tsp. smoked paprika
Salt and pepper, to taste
4-6 slices of bacon
Cooking spray

HOW TO COOK

1. Slice the jalapeño peppers lengthwise in half. Remove seeds and membranes.
2. Mix softened cream cheese, cheddar cheese, garlic, onion powder, smoked paprika, salt, and black pepper.
3. Fill each jalapeño half with the filling.
4. Wrap each jalapeño half with a slice of bacon, securing with a toothpick.
5. Preheat the air fryer to 375°F (190°C). Lightly spray the air fryer basket with oil spray.
6. Arrange the wrapped poppers in the basket in a single layer. Cook the for 10 to 12 minutes, until the bacon is crispy and the toppings are heated through.
7. Serve hot with creamy garlic sauce, sriracha mayonnaise, or guacamole.

NUTRITION INFO (Per Serving)

Calories: 350, Total Fat: 24.9 g, Saturated Fat: 11 g, Cholesterol: 79 mg, Sodium: 1107 mg, Total Carbs: 7.9 g, Fiber: 2 g, Sugar: 3 g, Protein: 20 g

Breakfast & Brunch

Ham Pepper Omelet

Servings: 1 • **Prep time:** 7 minutes • **Cook Time:** 12 minutes

If you love omelets, you will never have to worry about missing leftovers in your fridge. Any topping will go with it and in any combination you like. You can use fresh, lightly cooked, or even canned ingredients: vegetables and fruits, meat and fish, salty or sweet. An omelet is perfect without any sauce, but you can serve it with salsa, pesto, or Hoisin sauce. This hearty protein breakfast will energize you for the whole day without feeling heavy.

INGREDIENTS

2 whole eggs
1 Tbsp. heavy cream
2 Tbsp. Parmesan, shredded
¼ cup vegetables (bell peppers, onions, tomatoes, etc.), diced

2 Tbsp. ham, chopped
salt and pepper, to taste
olive oil spray

HOW TO COOK

1. Preheat your air fryer to 350°F (180°C).
2. Whisk eggs together with heavy cream, salt, and pepper. Mix in the fillings (e.g., vegetables, cheese, ham).
3. Spray a small oven-proof dish (that fits inside your air-fryer basket) with olive oil.
4. Pour the omelet mixture into the baking dish and place it in the air fryer basket.
5. Cook for 10 – 12 minutes.
6. Serve warm with crispy toasted bread.

NUTRITION INFO (Per Serving)

Calories: 174, Total Fat: 14.3 g, Cholesterol 186 mg, Sodium 165 mg, Total Carbohydrates 2.8 g, Dietary Fiber 0.2 g, Total Sugars 0.7 g, Protein: 9.7 g

French Toast Sticks

Servings: 1 • **Prep time:** 6 minutes • **Cook Time:** 8 minutes

Once a month, my Sunday morning starts with French toast sticks with whipped cream, a flavored latte, and orange juice. They are also great with currant jam or maple syrup. Crispy French toast with a soft crumb is quick and easy to make. I prefer white wheat bread as a base, but you can experiment with sweetbreads, whole-grain bread, or even gluten-free bread. Needless to mention, I don't have to convince my daughters to have a breakfast of toast with jam before their Sunday activities.

INGREDIENTS

2 bread slices, cut into 4 slices
1 whole egg
2 Tbsp. whole milk
¼ tsp. vanilla extract
1/8 tsp. cinnamon

½ tsp. light brown sugar
olive oil spray
liquid honey and fresh berries, for serving

HOW TO COOK

1. Preheat your air fryer to 350°F (180°C).
2. Whisk together egg, milk, vanilla extract, ground cinnamon, and sugar.
3. Coat each strip of bread with the egg mixture.
4. Lightly grease the basket of an air fryer with oil spray.
5. Arrange the bread strips in a single layer in the air fryer basket.
6. Cook the bread strips for 6-8 minutes until golden brown and crispy, flipping them halfway through.
7. Serve them with honey/ maple syrup or sprinkle with powdered sugar. Garnish with fresh berries to your liking.

NUTRITION INFO (Per Serving)

Calories: 250, Total Fat: 8 g, Cholesterol 8 mg, Sodium 380 mg, Total Carbohydrates 32 g, Dietary Fiber 2 g, Total Sugars 8 g, Protein: 13 g

Breakfast Sausages

Servings: 1 • **Prep time:** 7 minutes • **Cook Time:** 12 minutes

Traditional English breakfast is another tradition of our family, which I stick to even when my family is away, and I eat breakfast alone. It consists of fried sausages, fried eggs, toast, and fresh vegetables. I am happy to add vegetable stew if there is any leftover from dinner. It only takes 10-15 minutes to prepare and the simplest ingredients that you always have on hand. This hearty breakfast goes great with orange juice and flavored coffee.

INGREDIENTS

2 breakfast sausages (poultry/pork)
olive oil spray

HOW TO COOK

1. The recipe is easy to put into action even on busy mornings.
2. Preheat an air fryer to 350°F (175°C) for a few minutes.
3. Arrange the poultry/pork sausages in a single layer in the air fryer basket.
4. Air fry the sausages for 8-10 minutes, flipping them halfway through the cooking time.
5. Serve hot with your favorite garnishes. They perfectly pair with fried eggs, toasted bread, and fresh vegetables.

NUTRITION INFO (Per Serving)

Calories: 300, Total Fat: 26 g, Cholesterol 80 mg, Sodium 800 mg, Total Carbohydrates 2 g, Dietary Fiber 0 g, Total Sugars 0 g, Protein: 14 g

Potato Pancakes

Servings: 1 • **Prep time:** 10 minutes • **Cook Time:** 24 minutes

Pancakes are made with a simple batter that has plenty of room for improvisation: beat the egg and/or use cottage cheese to get light and airy pancakes, choose the type of flour, add grated vegetables (potatoes, zucchini, carrots, pumpkin).

Everyday pancake batter is ready in a flash, making it perfect for weekday breakfasts. Adjust the batter's consistency by adding milk or flour as needed. If possible, serve the pancakes at once; then they are the best.

INGREDIENTS

1 medium potato, peeled and grated
1 Tbsp. onion, chopped
1 small egg, beaten
1 Tbsp. whole milk
1 tsp. unsalted butter

1/8 tsp. garlic powder
1 Tbsp. all-purpose flour
Salt and pepper, to taste
Cooking spray

HOW TO COOK

1. Take a bowl and mix all the ingredients.
2. Preheat your air fryer to 375°F (190°C). Lightly grease the air fryer basket with cooking spray.
3. Divide the potato mixture into 2-3 equal portions. Shape each portion into a pancake or patty about 1/2-inch (7 mm) thick.
4. Arrange the potato pancakes in the air fryer basket in a single layer. Cook for 12-15 minutes until they are golden brown and crispy on both sides. Flip them halfway through.
5. Serve hot with your favorite sauce. Sour cream, Greek yogurt, horseradish sauce, or garlic aioli play well.

NUTRITION INFO (Per Serving)

Calories: 249, Total Fat: 9.9 g, Saturated Fat: 3 g, Cholesterol: 53 mg, Sodium: 470 mg, Total Carbs: 33 g, Fiber: 1 g, Sugar: 3 g, Protein: 6 g, Potassium: 672 mg

Bacon Wrapped Asparagus

Servings: 1 • **Prep time:** 10 minutes • **Cook Time:** 8 minutes

Asparagus is one of my favorite seasonal vegetables. I always buy it from local farmers. It is easy to prepare and can be cooked in a short time. The key is not to overcook it so that it doesn't get too soft. I often use it as a side dish. But if you wrap it in bacon, it becomes a complete snack or even breakfast. The bacon makes the dish more nourishing and adds juiciness and oiliness to the asparagus. Lemon zest, grated cheese, chopped fresh greens, chopped nuts, and toast go well with this dish.

INGREDIENTS

8 spears of asparagus, peeled and cut off the tough ends

4 bacon slices

1 Tbsp. sesame oil

1 garlic clove, crushed

Cooking spray

HOW TO COOK

1. Preheat your air fryer to 380°F (195°C).
2. Mix sesame oil and crushed garlic in a small bowl.
3. Wrap each two asparagus spears with a bacon slice.
4. Sprinkle wraps with garlic-oil mix, and place in the air fryer basket in a single layer.
5. Cook for 8 minutes, flipping once.
6. Bacon-wrapped asparagus can be a great addition to brunch, served with scrambled eggs, omelet, or quiche.
7. Serve hot with Hollandaise sauce, ranch dressing, or chimichurri sauce.

NUTRITION INFO (Per Serving)

Calories: 174, Total Fat: 15.9 g, Saturated Fat: 4 g, Cholesterol: 15 mg, Sodium: 327 mg, Total Carbs: 6, Fiber: 2 g, Sugar: 2 g, Protein: 5 g, Potassium: 280 mg

Seafood

Air-Fried Salmon with Salad

Servings: 1 • **Prep time:** 20 minutes • **Cook Time:** 9 minutes

Cooking fish is very simple - you need to add spices, fry or roast the fish, and sprinkle it with a wedge of lemon. And it is not even so important what kind of fish you cook. You just choose the kind that you like to taste. In addition, the fish cooks very quickly. Basically, after 5 minutes, the fish is ready.

Salmon is so delicious with a minimum of seasonings that you can add almost nothing. But if you do want it more complicated, leave the fish in the seasonings or marinade for up to 30 minutes. This will help bring out some of the flavors. My favorite flavorings for marinating fish are ground spices, dry herbs, mustard, lemon juice, or fragrant oils.

INGREDIENTS

1 salmon fillet (180 g) skin-on/skinless
1 lime wedge, for sprinkling
Olive oil spray

For the Marinade
1 tsp. olive oil
1 Tbsp. lemon juice
1 small garlic clove, crushed
1/8 tsp. dried rosemary
1/8 tsp. dried thyme
1/8 tsp. smoked paprika
salt and pepper, to taste

For the Salad
½ avocado, peeled and chopped
1 tomato (70 g), chopped
1 Tbsp. red onion, chopped
1 tsp. drained capers
1 Tbsp. olive oil
1 tsp. white wine vinegar
1/8 tsp. dried oregano
1 tsp. fresh parsley, chopped
1 tsp. fresh lemon juice
sea salt and black pepper, to taste

HOW TO COOK

1. Combine all the ingredients for the marinade and cover the salmon fillet with it. Let the salmon rest in the fridge for 15 minutes.
2. Meanwhile, preheat the air fryer to 400°F (205°C).
3. Lightly grease the air fryer basket with olive oil spray. Place the salmon fillet skin side down into a preheated air fryer. Cook for 8 minutes. As long as you don't overcook, the results will be crispy on the outside and juicy on the inside.
4. Combine all the ingredients for the fresh salad in a bowl.
5. Serve this flaky salmon with the salad and a lime wedge.

NUTRITION INFO (Per Serving)

Calories: 570, Carbs: 17 g, Chol: 78 mg, Sodium: 221 mg, Fat: 41.7 g, Protein: 38 g, Fiber: 9.4 g, Total Sugars: 4.5 g, Potassium: 1477 mg

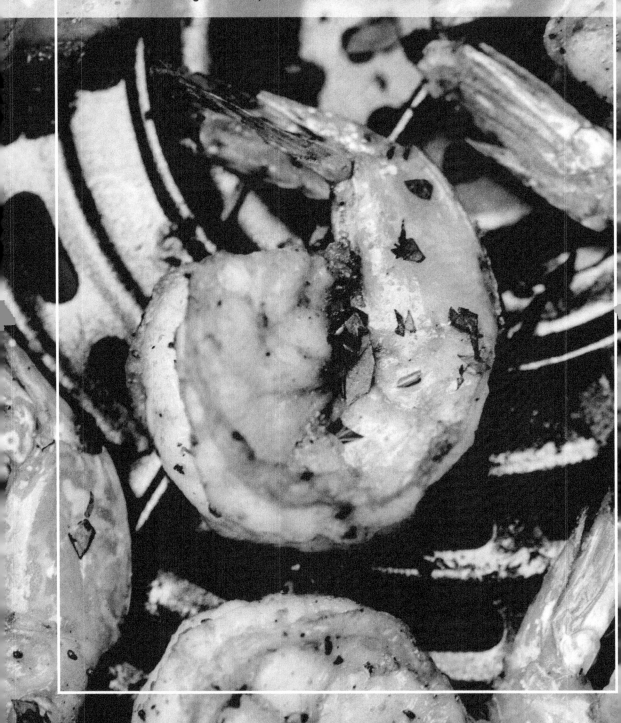

Garlic Shrimp

Servings: 1 • **Prep time:** 5 minutes • **Cook Time:** 12 minutes

Shrimp are the easiest of all seafood to prepare. You need to defrost them beforehand, add spices, and fry them for a few minutes. Even if you add just salt to them, it will bring out their natural flavor. But try them with other flavorings: ground spices, orange zest, tomatoes, garlic, chipotle, pesto, or curry. You can also fry them, coating them in batter, breadcrumbs, shredded coconut, or cornmeal. Only fry them for 2 -3 minutes more.

Serve shrimp with crusty bread as an ingredient for bruschetta or salad, over rice or pasta, or stuffed into tacos.

INGREDIENTS

½ lb. (225 g) raw shrimp
1 garlic clove, minced
1 Tbsp. fresh parsley, finely chopped
1 Tbsp. olive oil

1/8 tsp. fennel seeds
sea salt and black pepper, to taste
lemon wedge for sprinkling

HOW TO COOK

1. Preheat the air fryer to 400°F (205°C).
2. Meanwhile, toss shrimp with minced garlic, fennel seeds, olive oil, salt, and pepper.
3. Place the shrimp in a single layer in an air fryer basket. Cook for 10 – 12 minutes, depending on the size of your shrimp. Shake the basket once halfway through.
4. Sprinkle fried shrimp with chopped parsley and serve with a lemon wedge.

NUTRITION INFO (Per Serving)

Calories: 171, Total Carbohydrates: 2.9 g, Total Fat: 4.9 g, Cholesterol 238 mg, Sodium 277 mg, Protein: 26 g, Fiber: .0.4 g, Sugar: 0.3 g

Stuffed Flounder

Servings: 1 • **Prep time:** 8 minutes • **Cook Time:** 10 minutes

Flounder is a thin white fish that is easy to overcook. This means it's hard to make it crispy on the outside and juicy on the inside, which we all love. A great solution is to stuff it as a roll. That way, the crispy flounder on the outside will keep the stuffing juicy. I suggest a crab-meat and breadcrumbs filling. But I have other favorite fillings: feta with spinach, mushrooms with chopped fresh herbs, shrimp with cream cheese, or rice with vegetables.

Serve a flounder roll with a slice of lemon, fresh herbs, and fried nuts.

INGREDIENTS

1 flounder fillet
¼ cup breadcrumbs
salt and black pepper, to taste
2 Tbsp. crab meat (cooked/canned), crumbled

½ Tbsp. unsalted butter, melted
1 Tbsp. fresh parsley, finely chopped
½ Tbsp. lemon juice
Olive oil spray

HOW TO COOK

1. Preheat your air fryer to 375°F (190°C).
2. Flavor the fish fillet with salt and pepper, if needed.
3. Combine the fresh breadcrumbs, crab meat, chopped parsley, lemon juice, melted butter, sea salt, and pepper in a bowl.
4. Spread the stuffing over the flounder fillets. Be careful not to over-stuff. Roll the flounder on top of the stuffing to form a roll. Secure the ends of the flounder roll with toothpicks to keep the stuffing inside.
5. Lightly grease the fryer basket with cooking spray. Place the stuffed flounder roll in the basket. Cook the flounder for 8 - 10 minutes, until it is cooked through and the outside is crisp and golden.
6. Transfer the stuffed flounder to a serving platter and remove the toothpicks.
7. Serve hot with fresh seasonal salad or roasted vegetables.

NUTRITION INFO (Per Serving)

Calories: 289, Total Carbohydrates: 22.9 g, Total Fat: 8.9 g, Cholesterol 123 mg, Sodium 502 mg, Protein: 28 g, Fiber: .1.4 g, Sugar: 2.3 g

Roasted Scallops

Servings: 1 • **Prep time:** 7 minutes • **Cook Time:** 7 minutes

Cooking your own scallops is easy. The main caution in cooking fried scallops is not to overcook them. This problem is solved if you use an air fryer. And take care of the sauce. Scallops love creamy, buttery sauces like lemon butter sauce, creamy garlic sauce, tartar sauce, aioli, or a light mango salsa.

For a side dish, wild rice, garlic mashed potatoes, roasted asparagus, or fried Brussels sprouts would be great; the choice is yours.

INGREDIENTS

4 sea scallops
1 garlic clove, minced
1 tsp. orange/lemon juice
1 Tbsp. rosemary, chopped
1 Tbsp. olive oil/salted butter, melted

salt and pepper, to taste
1/8 tsp. smoked paprika
olive oil spray

HOW TO COOK

1. Preheat the air fryer to 400°F (205°C). Spray the basket lightly with oil.
2. Season scallops with salt and pepper and sprinkle with olive oil.
3. Place them in a single layer in the air fryer basket. Cook for 5 – 7 minutes, depending on the size of the scallops, flipping them once about halfway.
4. Combine orange/lemon juice, smoked paprika, chopped rosemary, melted butter, salt, and pepper.
5. Serve scallops with orange dressing and mashed broccoli.

NUTRITION INFO (Per Serving)

Calories: 122, Total Fat: 3 g, Cholesterol: 39 mg, Sodium: 185 mg, Total Carbohydrate: 4.9 g, Fiber: 1.4 g, Total Sugars: 0.3 g, Protein: 20 g

Fish and Chips

Servings: 1 • **Prep time:** 10 minutes • **Cook Time:** 27 minutes

Fans of America's classics will love this dish for lunch or even dinner. You can play with the breading: panko breadcrumbs, shredded coconut, chopped nuts and seeds, or rolled oats. Although these fried bites are good simply drizzled with lemon juice, you may prefer to dip them in sauces: salsa, pesto, garlic mayonnaise, tomato sauce, or ranch dressing are great accompaniments to fish and chips.

Fried food is the crispest immediately after cooking. Serve as soon as all the pieces are done. Garnish with fresh greens and lemon wedges on the side.

INGREDIENTS

For the Fish

1 white fish fillet (cod/haddock), cut into chunks

2 Tbsp. all-purpose flour

2 Tbsp. breadcrumbs

¼ tsp. smoked paprika

salt and pepper, to taste

1 whole egg, beaten

olive oil spray

For the Chips:

1 small potato, cut into strips

½ Tbsp. olive oil

Salt and pepper, to taste

HOW TO COOK

1. Preheat an air fryer to 400°F (200°C).
2. Place the all-purpose flour in one bowl. Combine the panko breadcrumbs, smoked paprika, salt, and pepper in another bowl.
3. Coat the fish chunks in the flour, then dip them in the beaten egg. Finally, coat the fillets with the seasoned breadcrumb mixture.
4. Drizzle the potato strips with olive oil, salt, and pepper.
5. Drizzle the air fryer basket with olive oil. Place the breaded fish fillets in the basket. Cook for 10-12 minutes until the fish is golden, turning it halfway through.
6. Take the fish from the air fryer and place the seasoned potatoes in the basket. Cook for 12-15 minutes until crispy and golden, shaking the basket occasionally.
7. Transfer the cooked fish and potato chips to a serving platter.
8. Serve hot with your choice of tartar sauce or lemon wedges.

NUTRITION INFO (Per Serving)

Calories: 452, Total Fat: 13 g, Cholesterol: 239 mg, Sodium: 250 mg, Total Carbohydrate: 54 g, Fiber: 3.4 g, Total Sugars: 2.3 g, Protein: 27 g

Poultry & Meat

Chicken Parmesan

Servings: 1 • **Prep time:** 8 minutes • **Cook Time:** 20 minutes

This is a dish you will never get tired of. It is very simple, quick to prepare, and consists of a winning combination of ingredients: chicken breast, cheese, and tomato sauce. In the recipe, the main flavor is taken over by Provencal herbs, but you can diversify the breading for chicken by adding chopped garlic or onions, mushrooms, chili, or lemon wedges. The breading allows you to retain the juices and fat inside. The chicken breast turns out juicy on the inside with a savory cheese crust.

Parmesan chicken pairs great with rice, pasta, fried or fresh vegetables. Serve hot or warm.

INGREDIENTS

For the Chicken:
1 chicken breast, boneless and skinless
2 Tbsp. all-purpose flour
2 Tbsp. breadcrumbs
2 Tbsp. Parmesan cheese, shredded
½ tsp. herbs de Provence
1 whole egg, beaten
olive oil spray

cooked spaghetti/pasta
salt and pepper, to taste

For the Topping:
2 Tbsp. Marinara sauce
2 Tbsp. mozzarella cheese, shredded
1 Tbsp. fresh parsley, chopped

HOW TO COOK

1. Preheat the fryer to 375°F (190°C).
2. Salt and pepper chicken breast.
3. Place the all-purpose flour in one bowl and the beaten egg in another. In a third bowl, combine breadcrumbs, grated Parmesan, and herbs.
4. Dip the chicken breast in the flour, then in the beaten egg, and finally in the breadcrumb mixture.
5. Lightly grease the fryer basket with cooking spray. Place the breaded chicken breast in the basket. Cook for 12-15 minutes, flipping halfway through.
6. When the chicken is almost done, drizzle with marinara sauce and mozzarella cheese. Cook for another 3-5 minutes until the cheese melts and bubbles.
7. Remove the chicken breast from the fryer and sprinkle with chopped parsley.
8. Serve the fried chicken Parmesan on a bed of spaghetti with a fresh seasonal salad.

NUTRITION INFO (Per Serving)

Calories: 731, Total Fat: 17 g, Cholesterol: 360 mg, Sodium: 601 mg,
Total Carbohydrate: 59 g, Fiber: 3.4 g, Total Sugars: 4.3 g, Protein: 76 g

Buffalo Chicken Wings

Servings: 1 • **Prep time:** 5 minutes • **Cook Time:** 17 minutes

Hot chicken wings originated in Buffalo, New York, hence the name Buffalo wings. Legend has it that Teressa Bellissimo of Anchor Bar figured out how she could quickly and easily feed her son and his friends. She deep-fried some chicken wings, dipped them in a mix of butter and hot sauce, and accompanied them with celery sticks and blue cheese dressing. The dish became popular in the area and eventually throughout the United States and beyond, becoming a favorite appetizer in bars, restaurants, and homes around the world.

INGREDIENTS

1 lb. (500 g) chicken wings
¼ cup (60 ml) cayenne pepper sauce
¼ cup (60 ml) coconut oil
1 tsp. Worcestershire sauce

½ tsp. garlic powder
½ tsp. sea salt
cooking spray

HOW TO COOK

1. Preheat your air fryer to 380°F (195°C).
2. Add cayenne pepper sauce, coconut oil, Worcestershire sauce, garlic powder, and some salt in a mixing bowl. Mix the buffalo sauce well and keep it on the side.
3. Pat the chicken dry with paper towels. Coat them evenly with the sauce.
4. Lightly grease an air fryer basket with a cooking spray.
5. Arrange the coated with the sauce chicken wings in a single layer in the basket.
6. Cook for 12 minutes at 380°F (195°C), flipping halfway through.
7. Increase the temperature to 400°F (205°C) and cook for 5 minutes more. They should be golden brown and crispy.
8. Remove the wings and transfer them to a serving platter.
9. Serve them with your favorite dipping sauce and celery sticks.

NUTRITION INFO (Per Serving)

Calories: 344, Total Fat: 19.9 g, Saturated Fat: 8 g, Cholesterol: 53 mg, Sodium: 366 mg, Total Carbs: 7 g, Fiber: 0 g, Sugar: 4 g, Protein: 8 g, Potassium: 141 mg

Breaded Chicken Thighs

Servings: 1 • **Prep time:** 15 minutes (plus 2-8 hours for marinating) • **Cook Time:** 12 minutes

Breading, keeping the bones inside and the skin, allows the poultry to retain its juiciness. For convenience, you can take pieces of chicken fillet and roll them in breading. It will also be delicious but will be less juicy. But they can be used as a snack on the go.

Your kids will demand these crispy chicken thighs over and over again. Serve them with baked potatoes, rice, pasta, and a fresh seasonal salad. Reheating makes them less crispy, but they remain just as juicy. The breaded thighs can be served with a variety of sauces, from tomato to creamy garlic and pesto.

INGREDIENTS

1-2 chicken thighs, skin-on and bone-in
¾ cup (180 ml) buttermilk
½ tsp. salt
1/3 tsp. cayenne pepper
¾ cup (100 g) all-purpose flour/
breadcrumbs

1 tsp. baking powder
1 tsp. garlic powder
1 tsp. paprika

HOW TO COOK

1. Rinse chicken thighs thoroughly and pat them dry, removing any fat residue.
2. Take a mixing bowl and add buttermilk, ½ teaspoon of paprika, half of cayenne pepper, and salt. Marinate the chicken in the mixture for 2 – 8 hours.
3. Preheat your air fryer to 400°F (205°C). Lightly grease an air fryer basket with olive oil or coconut oil.
4. Meanwhile, add flour, the rest of the paprika, cayenne pepper, garlic powder, and salt in another bowl.
5. Coat the chicken thighs with the flour mix and evenly arrange them in the air fryer basket. Cook for 12 minutes, flipping halfway through.
6. Serve with marinara sauce.

NUTRITION INFO (Per Serving)

Calories: 451, Total Fat: 13.9 g, Saturated Fat: 5 g, Cholesterol: 81 mg, Sodium: 356 mg, Total Carbs: 5 g, Fiber: 0 g, Sugar: 2 g, Protein: 25 g, Potassium: 303 mg

Chicken Kebab

Servings: 1 • **Prep time:** 10 minutes (plus 1-3 hours for marinating) • **Cook Time:** 15 minutes

In the Middle East, in the Ottoman Empire, the tradition of kebab originated, where meat was delicately roasted on a spit and served with bread and vegetables. Kebabs are made from lamb, beef, chicken, or fish. The meat is marinated, strung on skewers, and cooked over coals or gas flames. From the famous shish kebab to the beloved doner kebab to the flavorful kofta kebab, each differs in the combination of spices and cooking methods. Nowadays, kebabs are loved all over the world and are one of the staples of street food and fast food.

INGREDIENTS

1 lb. (450 g) chicken fillets, cut into 2" cubes

1 tsp. dried tarragon

2 tsp. olive oil

2 garlic cloves, minced

½ tsp. kosher salt

½ tsp. red pepper flakes

¼ tsp. black pepper

1/8 tsp. cayenne pepper

2 Tbsp. lemon juice

HOW TO COOK

1. Combine olive oil, lemon juice, dried tarragon, peppers, salt, and minced garlic in a bowl.
2. Marinate chicken chunks in the spice oil mixture for 30 – 60 minutes.
3. Preheat your air fryer to 400°F (204°C) and line the basket with parchment paper.
4. Meanwhile, thread the chicken chunks onto the skewers.
5. Arrange the skewers with the chicken chunks in the air fryer basket. Fry for 15 minutes. Ensure to flip halfway through the cooking time.
6. Serve with pita bread, rice, vegetables, or pickles. Kebab makes an ideal pairing with yogurt sauce, hummus, or baba ganoush.

NUTRITION INFO (Per Serving)

Calories: 250, Total Carbohydrates: 0.9 g, Total Fat: 11 g, Cholesterol 99 mg, Sodium 96 mg, Protein: 32.3 g, Fiber: 0.5 g, Sugar: 0.2 g

Honey Garlic Chicken

Servings: 1 • **Prep time:** 5 minutes (plus 30 minutes for marinating) • **Cook Time:** 15 minutes

This recipe draws inspiration from Chinese cuisine, at least American Chinese cuisine. It's a fusion dish that combines Chinese culinary techniques and American flavors of sweet and savory dishes. The caramelized sweetness of honey and lime pairs perfectly with the succulent and tender chicken. A recipe that's easy to bring to life even on busy evenings. The bright honey-spicy flavor of the chicken goes well with a neutral-flavored side dish - rice, vegetables, eggs, or noodles.

INGREDIENTS

2 chicken drumsticks, skinless
2 tsp. olive oil
2 tsp. liquid honey
½ tsp. garlic, minced

1 tsp. lime zest
1 tsp. lime juice
cooking spray

HOW TO COOK

1. To make the marinade, add olive oil, garlic, lime zest and juice, and honey to the mixing bowl. Whisk well.
2. Add chicken drumsticks and the marinade mixture to the zip bag and let it marinate for 30 minutes.
3. Preheat your air fryer to 400°F (205°C). Lightly oil the air fryer basket with a cooking spray.
4. Transfer the marinated chicken to the basket and cook for 15 – 20 minutes, flipping halfway through.
5. Garnish with rosemary sprigs. Serve with wild rice, fried vegetables, egg rolls, or Asian slaw.

NUTRITION INFO (Per Serving)

Calories: 481, Total Fat: 27.9 g, Saturated Fat: 7 g, Cholesterol: 245 mg, Sodium: 763 mg, Total Carbs: 4.9 g, Fiber: 1 g, Sugar: 4 g, Protein: 49 g, Potassium: 610 mg

Stuffed Chicken Breast

Servings: 1 • **Prep time:** 10 minutes • **Cook Time:** 18 - 20 minutes

A thin, tender chicken breast will be fine for stuffing. If you have bought it too thick, just lightly batter it to an even thickness before stuffing.

Bell peppers and mushrooms go well with cheese and chicken. Chop them finely and add them to the stuffing. For a spicy flavor, add fresh rosemary, thyme, or parsley.

INGREDIENTS

1 chicken breast (6 oz / 170 g), boneless,

¼ cup (1 oz. / 30 g) mozzarella cheese, shredded

2 sun-dried tomatoes, chopped (in oil, drained)

½ cup (15 g) fresh spinach, chopped

1 clove garlic, minced

1 tsp. olive oil

Salt and pepper to taste

fresh basil for garnish (optional)

HOW TO COOK

1. Preheat the air fryer to 375°F (190°C).
2. Slice the chicken breast horizontally to make a pocket, but be careful not to cut through it.
3. Heat 1 teaspoon of olive oil over medium heat in a small skillet.
4. Add the minced garlic and spinach and stir-fry until the spinach is soft, about 2 minutes. Remove from heat.
5. In a bowl, mix mozzarella cheese, sun-dried tomatoes, and roasted spinach.
6. Rub the inside of the chicken breast with salt and pepper.
7. Stuff the chicken breast with the mozzarella mixture and secure with toothpicks if necessary.
8. Lightly oil the air fryer basket with cooking spray.
9. Place the stuffed chicken breast in the basket of the air fryer.
10. Cook for 18 to 20 minutes until the internal temperature reaches 165°F (74°C) and the chicken is golden brown.
11. Remove the stuffed chicken from the air fryer and let it rest for a few minutes.
12. Garnish with fresh basil, if desired. Serve immediately.

NUTRITION INFO (Per Serving)

Calories: 320, Total Fat: 16 g, Cholesterol: 95 mg, Sodium: 480 mg, Total Carbs: 4 g, Fiber: 1 g, Sugar: 1.9 g, Protein: 37.9 g

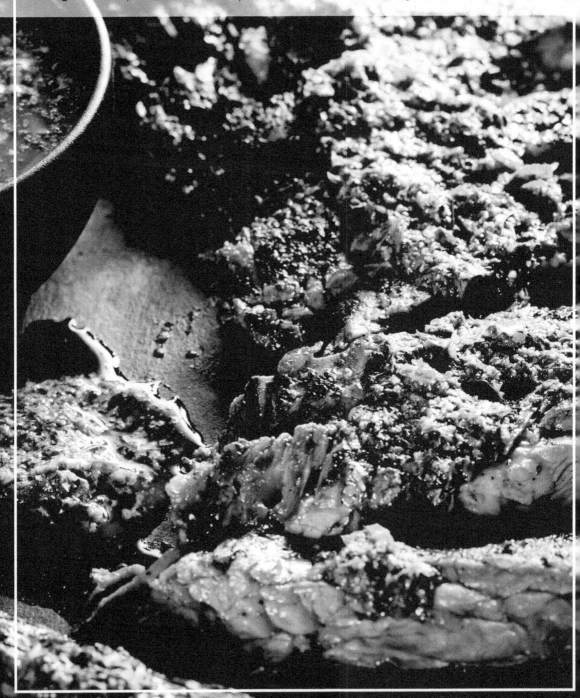

Skirt Steak with Chimichurri

Servings: 1 • **Prep time:** 10 minutes (plus 2-12 hours for marinating) • **Cook Time:** 10 minutes

A good steak is the right cut. Choose the best quality meat, and then it will be difficult to spoil it only if you overcook it to a degree you don't want. Skirt steak is traditionally marinated, but not for tenderness - the thin slices take care of that - but for flavor.

Serve the skirt steak with roasted potatoes, lime rice, sautéed mushrooms, or grilled corn. It can also be used as a salad ingredient.

INGREDIENTS

1 beef skirt steak (1-inch, 1 cm thick)
olive oil spray

Chimichurri Sauce
½ cup fresh parsley, finely chopped
1 Tbsp. fresh mint, finely chopped
1 Tbsp. fresh oregano, finely chopped
2 garlic cloves, minced

½ tsp. crushed red pepper
1 tsp. ground cumin
½ tsp. cayenne pepper
1 tsp. smoked paprika
½ tsp. sea salt
1/8 tsp. black pepper
¼ cup (180 ml) olive oil
1 Tbsp. red wine vinegar

HOW TO COOK

1. Add all the ingredients for the Chimichurri sauce to a bowl and mix them well.
2. Add ¼ cup of Chimichurri sauce and the steak in a resealable bag. Toss it to ensure the steak is coated well. Let it marinate in the fridge for 2-12 hours.
3. Remove the marinated steak from the refrigerator 30 minutes before cooking.
4. Preheat your air fryer to 390°F (200°C). Lightly coat the air fryer basket with olive oil spray.
5. Arrange the marinated steak in the air fryer basket and cook for 10-12 minutes (for 1″ steak) if you want a medium-rare finish. Flip halfway through.
6. Let the steak rest for 5-6 minutes on the cutting board, allowing the juices to redistribute throughout the meat.
7. Slice the steak across the fibers into thin slices. This will make it easier to chew and enjoy the flavor of the meat. Fan the slices for an attractive presentation.
8. Spoon the sauce over the steak and serve.

NUTRITION INFO (Per Serving)

Calories: 444, Total Fat: 17.9 g, Saturated Fat: 5 g, Cholesterol: 42 mg, Sodium: 276 mg, Total Carbs: 8.9 g, Fiber: 1 g, Sugar: 2 g, Protein: 13 g, Potassium: 262 mg

Breaded Schnitzel

Servings: 1 • **Prep time:** 10 minutes • **Cook Time:** 12 minutes

This is one of those classic dishes that we've all come to love cooking in the air fryer. Juicy meat in crispy breading pairs with about any side dish, from rice to mashed potatoes. But if you want something more sophisticated, add mushroom sauce, creamy mustard sauce, or hollandaise sauce. They are so versatile that you can easily serve them with almost any chicken, meat, or fish dish.

If you have enough time, serve the sauce with a side of sautéed spinach for a hearty dinner.

INGREDIENTS

1 thin beef schnitzel
2 Tbsp. olive oil
3 Tbsp. breadcrumbs
1/8 tsp. black pepper
a pinch of salt

1 whisked egg
1 lemon wedge, for garnish
parsley, for garnish
cooking spray

HOW TO COOK

1. Preheat your air fryer to 390°F (200°C). Lightly oil the air fryer basket with a cooking spray.
2. Take a bowl and mix breadcrumbs, salt, pepper, and olive oil.
3. Dip schnitzel into the whisked egg and dredge into the breadcrumbs.
4. Place the meat into the air fryer basket and cook for 12 minutes. Flip it halfway through.
5. Serve with a lemon slice and fried baby potatoes.

NUTRITION INFO (Per Serving)

Calories: 413, Total Fat: 10.9 g, Saturated Fat: 3 g, Cholesterol: 114 mg, Sodium: 506 mg, Total Carbs: 43 g, Fiber: 1 g, Sugar: 1 g, Protein: 33 g, Potassium: 590 mg

Parmesan-Crusted Pork Chops

Servings: 1 • **Prep time:** 7 minutes • **Cook Time:** 10 minutes

Pork, cheese, and spices are almost a holy combination. Frying pork chops in cheese breading is the easiest way to get succulent meat in a crispy, spicy crust. This dish is so self-sufficient that I recommend using only vegetables as a side dish: frying green beans, roasted Brussels sprouts, baked cabbage steaks with chopped nuts, or roasted asparagus.

Also, cheesy pork chops are a perfect ingredient for meal prep. They store well in the refrigerator. When reheated, the crust loses a little of its crispness but still has a nice texture and flavor soaked in the meat juices.

INGREDIENTS

1 thick pork chop, center-cut boneless
2 Tbsp. pork rind crumbs
1 small egg, beaten
2 Tbsp. Parmesan, grated
1/8 tsp. black pepper
1/8 tsp. smoked paprika

1/8 tsp. chili powder
1/4 tsp. onion powder
a pinch of salt
1 Tbsp. olive oil
oil spray

HOW TO COOK

1. Preheat your air fryer to 400°F (205°C). Coat the air fryer basket with oil spray.
2. Drizzle the pork chop with olive oil and season with salt and pepper.
3. Mix pork rind crumbs, Parmesan cheese, and spices in a bowl.
4. Pour the beaten egg into another bowl.
5. Dip the pork chop into the egg mix and then coat it with the crumb mix.
6. If you like a thick crust, make a double breading.
7. Place the breaded pork chop into the air fryer basket and fry for 10 – 12 minutes, flipping once halfway through.
8. Let it rest for 5 minutes before serving. Serve with green beans or Brussels sprouts.

NUTRITION INFO (Per Serving)

Calories: 271, Total Fat: 12 g, Total Carbs: 4 g, Fiber: 1 g, Protein: 27.9 g

Beef Lula Kebab

Servings: 1 • **Prep time:** 5 minutes • **Cook Time:** 10 minutes

Lula kebab is a popular Iranian dish made of minced meat. Its name comes from the Persian term for ground beef, which emphasizes its key ingredient. Legend has it that centuries ago, an Iranian merchant returning from India brought this savory dish to Iran, where it quickly won the hearts and tastes of the locals, becoming a cherished culinary tradition.

INGREDIENTS

6 oz. (170 g) minced beef/lamb
1 garlic clove, minced
1 small yellow onion (50 g), finely chopped
1/8 tsp. ground nutmeg
1/8 tsp. allspice

1/8 tsp. smoked paprika
⬚ tsp. black pepper
1/8 tsp. dried cumin
1/8 tsp. dried cardamom
1/8 tsp. kosher salt
cooking spray

HOW TO COOK

1. Combine all the ingredients in a bowl.
2. Use your hands to shape the mixture into 4 oval kebabs. Also, you can string the meat on skewers.
3. Preheat your air fryer to 350°F (178°C). Lightly coat an air fryer basket with a cooking spray.
4. Place the kebabs in the air fryer basket in a single layer. Cook for 12 minutes, flipping halfway through.
5. Don't overcook — they should be slightly pink inside, so they're still juicy!
6. Serve with naan and rice, or enjoy on their own.

NUTRITION INFO (Per Serving)

Calories: 153, Total Carbohydrates: 3 g, Total Fat: 4.9 g, Cholesterol 67 mg, Sodium 51 mg, Protein: 23.6 g, Fiber: 0.5 g, Sugar: 1.1 g

Sausage with Potato

Servings: 1 • **Prep time:** 15 minutes • **Cook Time:** 20 minutes

This dish is a model of simplicity, so complement it with bright sauces: chipotle mayo, chimichurri, BBQ sauce, or garlic aioli. So much flavor with so few ingredients. If you don't like dill as a garnish, try arugula or parsley.

INGREDIENTS

4 baby potatoes, halved
3 garlic cloves, squashed
1 Tbsp. fresh rosemary, chopped
3 slices diced bacon/ 2 chopped sausages

2 Tbsp. chopped fresh dill, for garnish
1 Tbsp. olive oil

HOW TO COOK

1. Mix garlic, bacon/sausages, potatoes, rosemary, and oil in a bowl.
2. Preheat your air fryer to 390°F (200°C).
3. Arrange the mixture in an air fryer basket in a single layer. Cook for 20 minutes until golden, shaking every 7 – 10 minutes.
4. Garnish with chopped dill.
5. Serve warm, accompanied with fresh vegetables for a satisfying dinner.

NUTRITION INFO (Per Serving)

Calories: 382, Total Fat: 13.9 g, Saturated Fat: 8 g, Cholesterol: 33 mg, Sodium: 527 mg, Total Carbs: 34 g, Fiber: 1 g, Sugar: 3 g, Protein: 6 g, Potassium: 798 mg

Steak Tacos

Servings: 1 • **Prep time:** 10 minutes • **Cook Time:** 10 minutes

Marinate the steak for 30 minutes before cooking for a richer flavor. If you are substituting steak for chicken breast or mushrooms, reduce the cooking time to 5 - 9 minutes. For charred flavor, increase the fryer temperature to 425°F (220°C) in the last 2 minutes of cooking.

Sauces that go great with tacos: Avocado sauce (1 ripe avocado, 2 tbsp. lime/lemon juice, 1/4 cup (60 g) Greek yogurt, 1 garlic clove, salt to taste), Salsa Verde (1 cup (240 ml) cooked tomatillos, 1/4 cup fresh cilantro, 1 de-seeded jalapeño, 1 garlic clove, 1/4 cup (60 ml) onion, salt to taste), or Chipotle Mayo (1/2 cup (120 ml) mayonnaise, 1-2 chipotle peppers in adobo sauce, 1 tbsp. lime juice).

INGREDIENTS

1 small flour or corn tortilla

4 oz. (115 g) steak/ chicken breast/ portobello mushrooms, thinly sliced

¼ cup cilantro, chopped

¼ cup onion, diced

1 Tbsp. olive oil

¼ tsp. garlic powder

¼ tsp. cumin

¼ tsp. smoked paprika

salt and pepper, to taste

1 lime wedge

2 Tbsp. avocado sauce or your favorite taco sauce

HOW TO COOK

1. Preheat an air fryer to 400°F (200°C).
2. Mix the sliced steak with olive oil, garlic powder, dried cumin, smoked paprika, salt, and black pepper.
3. Place the seasoned steak slices in the basket of the air fryer in a single layer.
4. Cook steak in preheated air fryer for 7-8 minutes, flipping halfway through, until meat is the desired doneness.
5. Reheat the tortilla in the air fryer for the last minute of cooking or in a skillet for 30 seconds on each side.
6. Place the cooked steak slices on a warm tortilla.
7. Sprinkle chopped cilantro, diced onion, and a squeeze of lime juice on top.
8. Drizzle with avocado sauce or your preferred taco sauce.

NUTRITION INFO (Per Serving)

Calories: 350, Total Fat: 18 g, Cholesterol: 70 mg, Sodium: 700 mg, Total Carbs: 20 g, Fiber: 2 g, Sugar: 2 g, Protein: 24.9 g

Sides & Vegetables

Cabbage Steaks

Servings: 1 • **Prep time:** 10 minutes • **Cook Time:** 18 minutes

When you are selecting a head of cabbage, it is good to check the outer leaves. They should be deep green or purple in color and firm to the touch but not stiff or crisp. If you find any damaged or wilted leaves, remove and discard them after washing the cabbage.

Crispy fried cabbage goes great with sauces and dips - hummus, tahini sauce, or ranch dressing. Try to add chopped bacon or toasted nuts. It makes this light dish heartier.

INGREDIENTS

¼ of head green/red cabbage (200 g), cut into 2 – 3 wedges/steaks
herbed oil spray
sea salt
¼ tsp. onion powder
¼ tsp. garlic powder

¼ tsp. black pepper
3 Tbsp. toasted pecans/ almonds, chopped
¼ cup Parmesan, grated
lemon wedges for garnish

HOW TO COOK

1. Preheat your air fryer to 400°F (204°C).
2. Spray cabbage steaks with herbed oil and season with garlic powder, onion powder, pepper, and salt.
3. Arrange cabbage steaks in an air fryer basket, ensuring that they do not overlap the pieces. Cook for 18 minutes or until tender and crispy, flipping halfway through.
4. Transfer the cabbage steaks to a serving platter. Sprinkle with toasted nuts and grated Parmesan, drizzle with lemon wedges.
5. Serve crispy cabbage steaks as a side, or add cooked chicken or pork for a tasty main dish. Or try fried eggs as a protein source.

NUTRITION INFO (Per Serving)

Calories: 189, Total Fat: 14.1 g, Cholesterol: 0 mg, Sodium: 49 mg, Total Carbohydrate: 16.9 g, Fiber: 7.1 g, Total Sugars: 7.2 g, Protein: 6 g

Fried Cauliflower

Servings: 1 • **Prep time:** 10 minutes • **Cook Time:** 8 minutes

When it comes to frying vegetables, you have two options - breaded or not. Cauliflower is fiber-rich, low in calories, and contains no cholesterol. The high-water content means you can count them among vegetables that help you lose or maintain a healthy weight.

No matter exactly how you cooked the broccoli, there are several last-minute additions that can make a big difference in the taste of the cooked dish: drizzle with lemon juice, sprinkle with fresh herbs/citrus zest or chopped nuts, drizzle with flavored oil, or sprinkle with spices.

INGREDIENTS

2 cups broccoli/cauliflower bite-sized florets

salt, and black pepper

½ tsp. dried rosemary

2 Tbsp. olive oil, divided

1 Tbsp. garlic powder, chopped

2 Tbsp. fresh parsley, chopped

2 lemon wedges, for garnish

HOW TO COOK

1. Preheat your air fryer to 375°F (190°C).
2. Toss broccoli/cauliflower florets with 1 tablespoon of olive oil, salt, pepper, rosemary, and garlic powder.
3. Arrange cauliflower in an air fryer basket in a single layer. Cook for 6 – 8 minutes to bring out the natural sweetness of the vegetable. Flip halfway through.
4. Sprinkle the fried cauliflower with chopped parsley and serve with lemon wedges.
5. Try it on its own or dressed with hummus or light mayo to create a fresh, healthy, and delicious side dish any time of year.

NUTRITION INFO (Per Serving)

Calories: 119, Total Carbohydrates: 9.1 g, Fat: 8 g, Protein: 4 g, Sodium 241 mg, Fiber: 3 g, Sugar: 2 g

Hasselback Potato

Servings: 1 • **Prep time:** 5 minutes • **Cook Time:** 20 minutes

An air fryer is simply indispensable for cooking hasselback potatoes. They turn out perfectly cooked, crispy, and cool-looking. Choose Russet potatoes, Yukon Gold, or sweet potatoes for the best combination of crispy crust and soft insides.

If you want something a little more gourmet, 5 minutes before the end of baking, take out the basket and insert a slice of cheddar cheese between each potato slice. Continue frying for another 5 minutes until the cheese is melted.

INGREDIENTS

2 medium/ 3 small Russet potatoes, washed and dried
1½ Tbsp. butter, melted
salt and black pepper, to taste

2 garlic cloves, minced
1 Tbsp. fresh rosemary, chopped, for garnish

HOW TO COOK

1. Preheat your air fryer to 400°F (204°C).
2. Slice the potato into thin slices, leaving the bottom whole without cutting through the tuber. The approximate slice thickness is 1/8 inch.
3. Mix melted butter, minced garlic, salt, and pepper in a small bowl.
4. Brush the potatoes liberally with the butter mixture, being mindful of the gaps between the slices.
5. Arrange potatoes in the air fryer basket and cook for 15 - 20 minutes.
6. Remove the basket and brush the potatoes with the butter mixture. Cook for 15 - 20 minutes more until golden brown and tender. Cooking time will be slightly longer for large potatoes.
7. Transfer the Hasselback potatoes to a serving platter, drizzle with the remaining garlic butter, and sprinkle with fresh rosemary.
8. Serve warm immediately for the crispiest crust.

NUTRITION INFO (Per Serving)

Calories: 311, Total Fat: 18 g, Cholesterol: 46 mg, Sodium: 137 mg,
Total Carbohydrate: 35.7 g, Fiber: 6.1 g, Total Sugars: 2.2 g, Protein: 4.2 g

Spicy Butternut Squash

Servings: 1 • **Prep time:** 10 minutes • **Cook Time:** 20 minutes

You can substitute butternut squash with pumpkin, carrots, sweet potato, or baby potato. In this case, you should adjust the cooking time. Or play with different spices and herbs in order to get a bright flavor.

Mix Greek yogurt, zest and juice of fresh orange and sumac to taste for a flavorful sauce to these spicy squash chunks.

INGREDIENTS

1 small butternut squash (1 lb./½ Kg), peeled and cubed

2 tsp. cumin seeds

1 tsp. chili flakes

1 Tbsp. olive oil/avocado oil

1½ oz. (40 g) pine nuts, toasted

3 Tbsp. fresh coriander, chopped

HOW TO COOK

1. Preheat your fryer to 360°F (185°C).
2. Meanwhile, mix chunked squash, spices, and oil in a bowl.
3. Place the spicy squash chunks in a single layer in the air fryer basket.
4. Cook for 20 minutes. Ensure to shake the basket every 6-8 minutes.
5. Transfer the fried squash to a serving platter and sprinkle with toasted pine nuts.

NUTRITION INFO (Per Serving)

Calories: 214, Total Fat: 14.9 g, Saturated Fat: 2 g, Cholesterol: 0 mg, Sodium: 1378 mg, Total Carbs: 20 g, Fiber: 22 g, Sugar: 7 g, Protein: 16 g, Potassium: 1370 mg

Stuffed Mushrooms

Servings: 5 mushrooms • **Prep time:** 10 minutes • **Cook Time:** 16 minutes

Do away with the usual side dishes today and complete your meal with stuffed mushrooms. You can eat them as an appetizer by adding ground chicken or sliced fried bacon to them. Or serve the mushrooms with your favorite protein for a special and delicious dinner. Foodies will love pairing stuffed mushrooms with potato or onion soup.

Choose mushrooms with voluminous and hollow caps so you can fit more stuffing in.

INGREDIENTS

5 button mushrooms
2 Tbsp. sun-dried tomatoes, chopped
2 Tbsp. breadcrumbs
1 spring onion, chopped

2 Tbsp. cream cheese
2 Tbsp. Parmesan, shredded
cooking spray

HOW TO COOK

1. Cut the stems from the mushrooms and scoop out the center. Chop them finely.
2. Combine the chopped stems, sun-dried tomatoes, breadcrumbs, cream cheese, shredded Parmesan, and chopped spring onion.
3. Fill the mushrooms with the stuffing.
4. Preheat your air fryer to 400°F (204°C). Lightly coat an air fryer basket with a cooking spray or olive oil.
5. Arrange the stuffed mushrooms in a single layer in the air fryer basket. Cook for 6 minutes.
6. Serve as a side, or add roasted chicken or pork for a tasty main dish.

NUTRITION INFO (Per Serving)

Calories: 64, Total Carbohydrates: 3.3 g, Total Fat: 4 g, Cholesterol 12 mg, Sodium 111 mg, Protein: 4.9 g, Fiber: 0.6 g, Sugar: 0.4 g

Chicken Stuffed Sweet Potato

Servings: 1 • **Prep time:** 5 minutes • **Cook Time:** 35 minutes

Stuffed sweet potatoes are convenient because they can be prepared ahead and assembled just before baking for a quick snack. For vegetarians, a version with black beans or roasted mushrooms instead of chicken would work well.

Instead of store-bought sauce, you can make homemade sauce by combining ½ cup (120 ml) hot sauce (such as Frank's RedHot), ½ teaspoon Worcestershire sauce, ½ cup (120 ml) unsalted butter, 1 tablespoon white vinegar, ¼ teaspoon garlic powder, ¼ teaspoon cayenne pepper/chili powder/ paprika, and ¼ teaspoon salt. Whisk the mixture and simmer for about 5 minutes, stirring occasionally. Allow it to cool to room temperature.

INGREDIENTS

1 medium sweet potato
½ cup (70 g) cooked chicken/beef/pork, shredded
1 tsp. hot sauce
¼ cup (30 g) shredded cheddar cheese/ crumbled blue cheese/ cheddar and

mozzarella
1 tsp. red onion, finely chopped
1 tsp. olive oil
1 Tbsp. sour cream
1 Tbsp. chives, chopped
Salt and pepper to taste

HOW TO COOK

1. Preheat your air fryer to 400°F (200°C).
2. Pierce the sweet potato around with a fork in several places. Coat the skin with olive oil and season with salt and pepper.
3. Place the sweet potato in the basket of an air fryer and cook for 30-35 minutes until tender and cooked through.
4. While the potato is cooking, mix the shredded chicken, half of the cheddar, and half of the red onion in a small bowl. Season with salt and pepper.
5. When the sweet potato is cooked and tender, let it cool slightly. Make a slit in the middle and mash the inside with a fork.
6. Stuff the sweet potato with the chicken mixture. Sprinkle the remaining cheddar cheese and red onion on top.
7. Return the stuffed potato to the air fryer and cook for another 3-5 minutes until the cheese is melted and bubbling.
8. Remove from air fryer, drizzle with hot sauce, and sprinkle with sour cream and chopped chives.
9. Serve immediately and enjoy!

NUTRITION INFO (Per Serving)

Calories: 350, Carbohydrates: 38 g, Cholesterol: 60 mg, Sodium: 450 mg, Protein: 22 g, Fats: 14 g, Sugar: 9 g, Fiber: 6 g

Zucchini Open Tart

Servings: 1 • **Prep time:** 10 minutes • **Cook Time:** 12 - 15 minutes

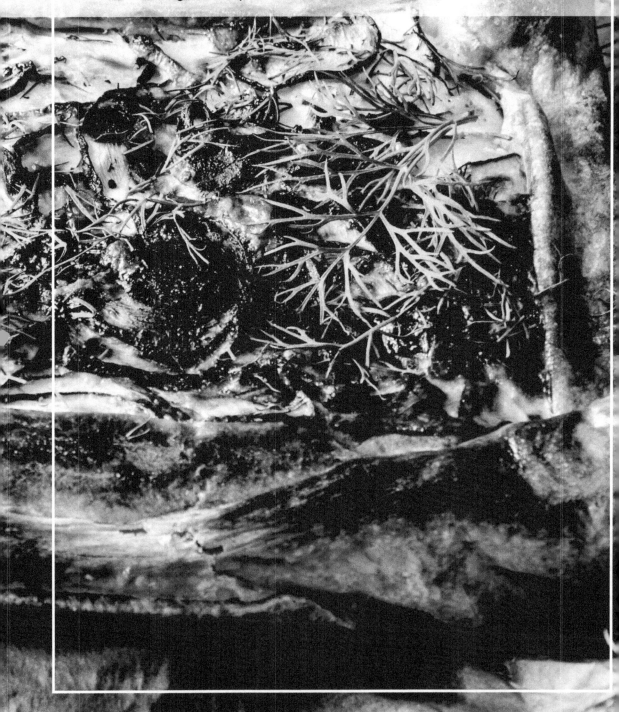

If it seems like fresh, flavorful baked goods are impossible when you need a quick snack alone, this recipe disproves that. You simply take an appropriately sized sheet of puff pastry and fill it with your favorite filling from the fridge. I like to add tomatoes and mushrooms and experiment with cheeses and herbs. The main thing is not to go overboard with the filling. If you like a crispy crust, bake the dough for 5 minutes beforehand and then add the filling.

INGREDIENTS

1 sheet puff pastry, thawed

1 small zucchini (½ cup / 75 g), thinly sliced

1 large egg

¼ cup (60 ml) heavy cream / double cream

¼ cup (30 g) Parmesan cheese, grated

1 clove garlic, minced

1 Tbsp. fresh dill, chopped

1 Tbsp. olive oil

Salt and pepper to taste

HOW TO COOK

1. Set the air fryer temperature to 350°F (180°C).
2. Roll out the puff pastry on a lightly floured surface. Fold the edges inward to create a small border.
3. In a small bowl, whisk together the egg, heavy cream, Parmesan cheese, crushed garlic, salt, and pepper.
4. Place the rolled puff pastry on a piece of parchment paper suitable for the fryer basket. Arrange the zucchini slices evenly over the dough. Pour the cream mixture over the zucchini, spreading it evenly.
5. Carefully transfer the parchment paper with the tart to the basket of the air fryer. Drizzle with olive oil. Cook for 12-15 minutes until the pastry is golden brown and the filling is set.
6. Remove the tart from the air fryer and let it cool slightly. Sprinkle with fresh dill before serving.

NUTRITION INFO (Per Serving)

Calories: 350, Carbohydrates: 38 g, Cholesterol: 60 mg, Sodium: 450 mg, Protein: 22 g, Fats: 14 g, Sugar: 9 g, Fiber: 6 g

Desserts

French Clafoutis

Servings: 2 ramekins • **Prep time:** 7 minutes • **Cook Time:** 30 minutes

Clafoutis is a fancy French dessert that originates from the Limousin region in the heart of France. It is made by mixing eggs, milk, sugar, and flour to form a batter, poured over a bed of sweet, juicy cherries, and then baked to perfection. The result is a creamy, custardy treat with a touch of nutty sweetness, perfectly complemented by the burst of cherries. Dust it with delicate powdered sugar and serve it warm for a summery treat that will transport you to a Parisian café!

INGREDIENTS

2 Tbsp. all-purpose wheat flour
1 small egg
2 Tbsp. whole milk
1 Tbsp. light brown sugar

1/8 tsp. vanilla extract
¾ cup fresh cherries
a pinch of salt
powdered sugar for sprinkling

HOW TO COOK

1. Preheat your air fryer to 320°F (160°C).
2. Grease two 8-ounce ramekins with butter.
3. Place cherries at the bottom of the ramekin.
4. Whisk together all remaining dessert ingredients and pour the mixture over the cherries.
5. Arrange ramekins in an air fryer basket and cook for 30 minutes until golden brown.
6. Sprinkle with powdered sugar and serve warm.

NUTRITION INFO (Per Serving)

Calories: 231, Total Fat: 3.4 g, Cholesterol: 85 mg, Sodium: 61 mg,
Total Carbohydrate: 44.3 g, Fiber: 0.7 g, Total Sugars: 11.8 g, Protein: 5.3 g

Bread Pudding

Servings: 2 ramekins • **Prep time:** 7 minutes • **Cook Time:** 30 minutes

You can use white flour bread, whole-wheat bread, ciabatta, French bread, brioche, or challah as a base. Ensure to dry out fresh bread by toasting it in the oven before using.

You can make your vanilla pudding sauce. Whisk milk, brown sugar, oil, egg, flour, cinnamon, and salt in a bowl until smooth. Cook in a saucepan over medium heat, whisking constantly, until the sauce thickens, 10 to 12 minutes. Add vanilla extract. Gourmets can substitute vanilla extract for rum or Bourbon.

INGREDIENTS

1 cup dry whole wheat bread/French bread, cubed
½ cup mango, cubed
2 Tbsp. candied fruits, chopped
1 small egg
½ cup whole milk/coconut milk
1 Tbsp. light brown sugar

1/8 tsp. vanilla extract
1/8 tsp. cinnamon
1/8 tsp. nutmeg
a pinch of salt
cooking spray
powdered sugar for sprinkling

HOW TO COOK

1. Preheat your air fryer to 350°F (180°C).
2. Coat two 8-ounce ramekins with cooking spray.
3. Place bread cubes, mango, and candied fruits at the bottom of the ramekins.
4. Whisk together all the remaining ingredients for the pudding and pour the mixture over the bread. Let it stand for 5 minutes.
5. Arrange ramekins in an air fryer basket and cook for 15 minutes until set.
6. Serve warm with your favorite sauce.

NUTRITION INFO (Per Serving)

Calories: 283, Total Fat: 7.4 g, Cholesterol: 185 mg, Sodium: 311 mg, Total Carbohydrate: 39 g, Fiber: 4.7 g, Total Sugars: 19.8 g, Protein: 13.3 g

Stuffed Apple

Servings: 1 apple • **Prep time:** 5 minutes • **Cook Time:** 20 minutes

Baked apples are a favorite treat and a great way to incorporate fruit into your diet. They are perfect for snacks and lunches and are also a healthy dessert. To make them a complete snack, you can increase their nutritional value by adding rolled oats.

Stuffed apples topped with vanilla ice cream, caramel sauce, or whipped cream make a delicious dessert combination.

INGREDIENTS

1 apple (Granny Smith, Gala, Honey Crisp), cored, but leave a bottom

For the Stuffing:
1 Tbsp. honey
1 tsp. unsalted butter
1 Tbsp. walnuts/pecans, crushed

1 Tbsp. raisins/dried cranberries/dried apricots
1/8 tsp. ground cinnamon
1/8 tsp. ground cardamom

HOW TO COOK

1. Mix together all the ingredients for the stuffing. Spoon the stuffing into the hole in the apple.
2. Place the apple into the air fryer basket and cook for 20 minutes at 350°F (180°C) until the apple is soft.
3. Serve with vanilla ice cream or drizzle with caramel sauce.

NUTRITION INFO (Per Serving)

Calories: 291, Total Fat: 8.7 g, Cholesterol: 10 mg, Sodium: 31 mg,
Total Carbohydrate: 56.3 g, Fiber: 6.7 g, Total Sugars: 45.4 g, Protein: 2.9 g

Fried Peaches

Servings: 1 • **Prep time:** 5 minutes • **Cook Time:** 10 minutes

Customize the toppings for warm peaches to your desire. The combination of vanilla ice cream, melted chocolate, and peaches is divine. For a creamy contrast, try adding yogurt or whipped cream. A gentle drizzle of honey and cinnamon enhances the sweetness and warmth of the dish. Granola or nuts add texture to each bite.

INGREDIENTS

2 peaches/4-6 apricots, pitted and halved
½ tsp. honey
1 tsp. butter

1/8 tsp. cinnamon
1 Tbsp. almonds/pecans, finely chopped

HOW TO COOK

1. Preheat your air fryer to 375°F (190°C). Line an air fryer basket with parchment paper.
2. Drizzle peach/apricot halves with honey, sprinkle with cinnamon and chopped nuts, and top with a piece of butter.
3. Place the peaches' skin down into the air fryer basket. Cook for 10 minutes until tender.
4. Transfer the peaches to a serving platter and drizzle with caramel sauce. Serve with vanilla ice cream.

NUTRITION INFO (Per Serving)

Calories: 203, Total Fat: 7.7 g, Cholesterol: 10 mg, Sodium: 27 mg, Total Carbohydrate: 33 g, Fiber: 5.7 g, Total Sugars: 32 g, Protein: 3.9 g

Mini Brownie

Servings: 1 • **Prep time:** 5 minutes • **Cook Time:** 12 minutes

This chocolate fudge makes your mouth water. It is quick and easy to prepare, and even beginners can make it. Add chocolate drops and cinnamon for a more sophisticated flavor. Drizzle chocolate or raspberry sauce over cooked brownies and sprinkle with coconut shavings or crushed nuts. Serve with whipped cream, a scoop of ice cream, berries, or raisins.

INGREDIENTS

2 Tbsp. all-purpose flour
2 Tbsp. butter/coconut oil, melted
2 Tbsp. sugar
1 Tbsp. cocoa powder

¼ tsp. vanilla extract
salt to taste
cooking spray

HOW TO COOK

1. Preheat your air fryer to 350°F (180°C). Lightly oil the ramekin with a cooking spray.
2. Mix all ingredients for the brownie in a small bowl until smooth.
3. Pour the batter into the ramekin. Cook for 10 – 12 minutes until set.
4. Let it cool, and serve it with a cup of milk.

NUTRITION INFO (Per Serving)

Calories: 296, Total Fat: 24 g, Cholesterol: 61 mg, Sodium: 165 mg, Total Carbohydrate: 21 g, Fiber: 2 g, Total Sugars: 8.4 g, Protein: 2.5 g

Banana Cake

Servings: 1 • **Prep time:** 5 minutes • **Cook Time:** 12 minutes

If you're a fan of baking in a mug, you'll love this easy banana cake recipe. If you want something sweet and quick, this is the solution. You can add chocolate drops, crushed nuts, or raisins to the batter. Try to use maple syrup as a substitute for brown sugar. Wheat flour can easily be substituted with coconut flour or almond flour.

Serve drizzled with peanut or nut butter or even with a scoop of your favorite ice cream.

INGREDIENTS

½ ripe banana, mashed
2 Tbsp. all-purpose flour
1 Tbsp. brown sugar
¼ tsp. baking powder

1/8 tsp. cinnamon
a pinch of salt
cooking spray
1 Tbsp. chocolate chips, for garnish

HOW TO COOK

1. Preheat your air fryer to 350°F (175°C). Lightly oil the ramekin with a cooking spray.
2. Mix all ingredients for the cake in a small bowl until smooth.
3. Pour the batter into the ramekin. Cook for 6 – 8 minutes until set.
4. Let it cool, and serve it with a cup of milk.

NUTRITION INFO (Per Serving)

Calories: 184, Total Fat: 4.7 g, Cholesterol: 3 mg, Sodium: 14 mg, Total Carbohydrate: 34.3 g, Fiber: 2.3 g, Total Sugars: 17.4 g, Protein: 2.9 g

7-DAY MEAL PLAN

MONDAY

Breakfast	Ham Pepper Omelet 26
Lunch	Air-Fried Salmon with Salad 38
Dinner	Chicken Parmesan 50 with Spicy Butternut Squash 82
Snacks	Potato Wedges 14
Desserts	French Clafoutis 92

TUESDAY

Breakfast	French Toast Sticks 28
Lunch	Garlic Shrimp 40 with Zucchini Open Tart 88
Dinner	Skirt Steak with Chimichurri 62 and Hasselback Potato 80
Snacks	Nut Cocktail 18
Desserts	Bread Pudding 94

WEDNESDAY

Breakfast	Breakfast Sausages 30
Lunch	Stuffed Flounder 42 with Fried Cauliflower 78
Dinner	Breaded Chicken Thighs 54 with Stuffed Mushrooms 84
Snacks	Onion Rings 20
Desserts	Stuffed Apple 96

THURSDAY

Breakfast	Potato Pancakes 32
Lunch	Beef Lula Kebab 68 with Cabbage Steaks 76
Dinner	Honey Garlic Chicken 58 with Chicken Stuffed Sweet Potato 86
Snacks	Jalapeño Poppers 22
Desserts	Fried Peaches 98

FRIDAY

Breakfast	Bacon Wrapped Asparagus 34
Lunch	Roasted Scallops 44 with Zucchini Open Tart 88
Dinner	Parmesan-Crusted Pork Chops 66 with Spicy Butternut Squash 82
Snacks	Mozzarella Sticks 16
Desserts	Mini Brownie 100

SATURDAY

Breakfast	Ham Pepper Omelet 26
Lunch	Fish and Chips 46 with Cabbage Steaks 76
Dinner	Stuffed Chicken Breast 60 with Hasselback Potato 80
Snacks	Nut Cocktail 18
Desserts	Banana Cake 102

SUNDAY

Breakfast	French Toast Sticks 28
Lunch	Chicken Kebab 56 with Fried Cauliflower 78
Dinner	Steak Tacos 72 with Stuffed Mushrooms 84
Snacks	Potato Wedges 14
Desserts	French Clafoutis 92

FROM THE AUTHOR

Christopher Lester, a culinary wizard and flavor magician, has cast a spell on the food world with his one-of-a-kind cooking techniques. With an arsenal of tools and tricks learned from some of the greatest names in the culinary kingdom, he creates dishes that are not only healthy but bursting with flavor.

When he's not whipping up culinary masterpieces in the kitchen, he's busy playing with his two daughters and his trusty kitchen companion, Jack, the dog. He loves to put on his apron in his spare time, gather his friends and family around the table, and treat them to feasts that make their taste buds dance with joy.

WHAT TO READ NEXT

Air Fryer Cookbook: Quick, Easy, and Delicious Air Fryer Recipes for Healthy and No-Fuss Cooking

Mediterranean Air Fryer Cookbook: Fun and Healthy Way to Cook Heart-Healthy Recipes in Your Air Fryer

Made in the USA
Las Vegas, NV
03 January 2025

15676826R00063